PARENTS' GUIDE TO

PRIMARY SCHOOLS

AND THE

NATIONAL CURRICULUM

Key Stages 1 and 2

Jim Sweetman

Contents

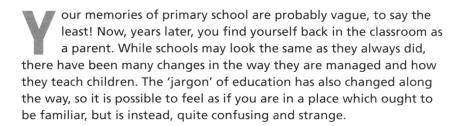

1 How this guide will help you

THE DIFFERENCE IN EDUCATION TODAY

' Schools have to follow new rules, on subjects as varied as sex education and swimming '

Your memories of primary school are probably vague, to say the least! Now, years later, you find yourself back in the classroom as a parent. While schools may look the same as they always did, there have been many changes in the way they are managed and how they teach children. The 'jargon' of education has also changed along the way, so it is possible to feel as if you are in a place which ought to be familiar, but is instead, quite confusing and strange.

When most of today's parents were at primary school, the education system was fairly straightforward. Basically, you sent your child to the school nearest to you. There was rarely any choice unless you opted for a denominational school (Church of England or Catholic) or paid for your child to attend an independent (private) school. Schools were managed by the Local Education Authority (LEA), which took a major role in appointing the governors, the headteacher and staff, looked after the school meals, buses, etc., and controlled the purse-strings. By and large, the decisions about what should be taught in the school were left to the headteacher and his or her staff. Occasional parents' evenings and brief school reports were the only ways in which parents found out how their children were getting on.

All this has changed. Schools now:
- are run by the governing body, headteacher and staff, working as a team
- are responsible for managing their own budgets
- must follow the teaching programmes set down in the National Curriculum
- have to follow new rules on subjects as varied as sex education and swimming
- can be compared with other schools via national assessments of pupils
- must publish a school prospectus and annual report
- are subject to inspections which report on how successful their programmes of teaching are

Some schools are no longer responsible to the LEA and manage themselves.

Parents now have responsibilities too. They are expected to choose a school and be much more involved in their children's education. Parents are now entitled, by law, to information about the school, via its prospectus and annual report.

This may seem quite daunting to the parent who wants to be positively involved in his or her child's education but is not quite sure how to set about it. This guide is designed to help you. It provides the basic information that will let you talk the same language as the teachers in your child's school and understand what they mean when they talk about the curriculum, your child's progress, or his or her test results. Involvement means anything from being able to discuss different subjects with your child's teacher at a parents' evening, to asking the headteacher about how the school's test results compare with the school down the road, or joining the governing body and helping to influence the development of the school. And, of course, involving yourself in your child's work at home may play a crucial part in his or her chances of success.

Finally, this guide does not assume that you know a great deal about schools and education. Instead, it starts with the belief that you are interested in how your children are educated and want to understand what is happening in their primary schools.

Summing up

- There have been major changes in schools since today's parents were pupils
- Most schools are obliged to follow the National Curriculum
- Schools now have much more responsibility

2 Primary education

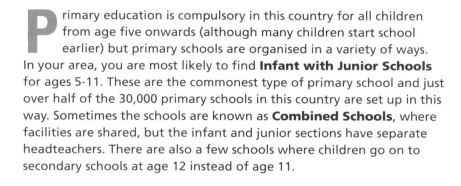

THE CHOICE AVAILABLE

'Private schools do not have to follow the National Curriculum'

Primary education is compulsory in this country for all children from age five onwards (although many children start school earlier) but primary schools are organised in a variety of ways. In your area, you are most likely to find **Infant with Junior Schools** for ages 5-11. These are the commonest type of primary school and just over half of the 30,000 primary schools in this country are set up in this way. Sometimes the schools are known as **Combined Schools**, where facilities are shared, but the infant and junior sections have separate headteachers. There are also a few schools where children go on to secondary schools at age 12 instead of age 11.

However, you could find that in your area **Infant Schools** operate from ages 5-7 and then children go on to a **Junior School** from ages 7-11. The smaller infant schools tend to be uneconomic to run and under 3,000 of each kind remain open. Lastly, in a few areas, there are still **Middle Schools** taking children from either ages 8-12 or 9-13. These schools are served by **First Schools** which take pupils aged 5-8 or 5-9. Because of the way the National Curriculum is structured, some of these schools are now being reorganised along infant and junior lines.

The vast majority of these schools are part of a **Local Education Authority (LEA)**. An LEA can be a department of a county, a metropolitan district or a borough council. It is ultimately responsible for all of the primary schools in its area, except for grant-maintained and independent schools. Denominational schools – almost entirely Church of England or Catholic – have what is known as 'controlled' or 'voluntary-aided' status. They have an extra degree of independence, but work closely with the Local Education Authority. **Grant-maintained schools** have opted out of local authority control. There are very few of them at primary level. They receive their funds directly from central government and, in theory at least, have greater flexibility over how they spend their money.

There are also about 1,000 **private**, or **independent**, infant, or infant and junior, schools in the United Kingdom. Sometimes these are known as **Preparatory Schools**, because they prepare children for public school. The main point to remember about private schools, apart from the fact that they charge fees, is that they do not have to follow the National Curriculum.

The size of primary schools varies. A small infant school can have less than 100 pupils, but a large infant and junior school can have as many as 400. Small schools can suffer from a lack of resources and specialist teaching, while large schools can be impersonal. As a rule, however, the size of a school tells you very little about how successful it is in comparison to its policy on selection, location and how it is managed.

HOW PRIMARY SCHOOLS ARE RUN

Every school has a **headteacher** and a **school secretary**. Larger schools have a **deputy headteacher** as well. Class teachers with responsibility for subjects like English, Mathematics and Science are known as **co-ordinators**. Schools often have co-ordinators for children with special needs and for supporting new subjects such as Information Technology, (IT, or computer work). In general, the larger the school, the more specialists it will support. On average, there should be about one teacher for every 25 pupils, but this does not mean that all classes will have that number of pupils. There is a lot of debate about class sizes and some evidence that smaller classes benefit the pupils in them. There is also agreement that teachers need time free for preparation if they are to work effectively.

The school will also have a **governing body,** made up of nine or ten people who work with the headteacher and look after the welfare of the school. All major decisions about the development of the school, including expenditure on new projects and the appointment of teachers, come under the control of the governors. Their leader, the chair of governors, is a very influential figure in a primary school, with almost as much power as the headteacher. At least two or three of the governors will have children at the school.

ADMISSION POLICIES

School admission policies vary. By law, children must attend a primary school from the first day of term following their fifth birthday. However, for many years, schools have admitted children at the start of the term in which their birthday falls. With the decline in school numbers in the last ten years, many schools have admitted children who are even younger – often at the beginning of the school year in which they are five. These children are known as 'rising-fives'. In many schools, rising-fives attend school for half days only, when they first start. The classes for the youngest children in the school are often known as **reception classes**. They may be organised less formally than the rest of the school and finish lessons earlier.

Summing up

What you need to know
- **How the schools are organised in your local area – Infant and Junior (5-11 or 12); Infant (5-7) and Junior (7-11); or First (5-8 or 9) and Middle (8 or 9 – 12 or 13)**
- **If there are any independent or grant-maintained alternatives**
- **Local school admission policies**

How to find out
- **Write to, or telephone, the Local Education Authority for school details**
- **Talk to other parents about independent or grant-maintained provision**
- **Watch for advertising in the local newspapers in late autumn or early spring**

3 Choosing a primary school

DO YOU HAVE A CHOICE?

The most important decision parents make in their children's education is the selection of a school. Depending on where you live, the process can be very straightforward or extremely complicated. Where there is a system of infant and junior schools, a choice may have to be made twice within a three-year period.

The first issue for parents is to decide whether or not there is a genuine choice to be made. If the local primary school is close to home, representative of the area (in the sense that the pupils come from similar homes) and situated in reasonable buildings, then there is probably no need to look further. There is no point in sending a young child on a long journey to a school in unfamiliar surroundings unless there is a good reason. Even where you think that a school has weaknesses, the benefits of being situated in the local area may outweigh them.

' There is no point in sending a young child on a long journey to school unless there is a good reason '

Making a choice may be important where there are two schools within the same approximate distance, or where there are denominational or independent schools in competition with the local school(s). In these situations, you will probably hear stories about the different primary schools, but it is important to make up your own mind and not be swayed by local gossip.

Where there are two local authority-maintained schools within the same approximate travelling time (a more useful guide than just the distance) then you will have to make a choice. To do this, you need to think about the sort of school you want your children to attend. Bear in mind that younger brothers and sisters will nearly always have the right to attend the same school as their older siblings, so this may be a decision which affects all of your children.

Find out as much information as you can to help you compare the schools. The documents you will need are the most recent **school prospectus** and the **annual report of the governing body**. If possible, visit the schools on your shortlist as well. It is not essential, but calling at the school to ask for the prospectus and report and to arrange a visit will give you an immediate indication of how welcoming the school is when it is working rather than on show!

' Remember that a good prospectus is an advertisement for the school '

As you read the prospectus, think about the overall impression it gives of the school. Does it come across as a caring place? Is there enough emphasis on the basics of literacy and numeracy? What are the buildings like? What is said about extra-curricular activities such as sports training, music and visits? Remember that a good prospectus is an advertisement for the school, so try to read between the lines. Is provision for swimming lessons mentioned? Does what is said about sex education, discipline, uniform and religion tie in broadly with your own views and beliefs? Finally, does the prospectus describe the school and its organisation in a way that makes it accessible to you as the parent of a potential pupil?

As you read the report of the governing body, check whether what the prospectus says has been carried into action. For example, if the prospectus says that the school is emphasising the use of computing, look to see whether the school has appointed an IT co-ordinator, is spending money on new machines or is dedicating a room for computer use. The results of last year's Key Stage 1 and 2 National Tests will be published and sent to the parents of prospective pupils. A summary of the school's results will be published in its prospectus along with national and local statistics. Look at what the school says about its academic performance and at how the school's test results compare with the national averages and the local figures. Look to see what is said about opportunities for staff development and training.

VISITING THE SCHOOL

All the impressions you get from your reading can be used to help you make the most of your visit. This will often be on some kind of school open day or evening and it is important to target the information you want to find out. When you see the computers on display in a class library area, ask where pupils normally work with them. It could be a cupboard! Talk to as many of the teachers as you can and try to gauge their enthusiasm. Asking about facilities for sport or music can tell you whether the staff work as a team and have a joint understanding of what the school is aiming to achieve. Asking classroom teachers about school policies can tell you if there is agreement among the staff on issues like marking or uniform.

In classrooms, look for examples of work displayed in interesting ways. Are there colourful books available for children to use regularly? How is the classroom arranged – is it formal or friendly? Are there reading areas and places for practical work within the room? Look at the fabric of the school. Even if worn, is it cared for? Are the walls clean even if the paint is fading? Do the flower beds look as if they have been raked over for the day, or are they always that neat? Are play areas safe and clean or is there evidence that they are vandalised at night by older children? Are there helpful signs that show you where to go in the school?

Of course, not all schools can put on the same kind of show for visitors. Do not expect a small infant school to have as glossy a prospectus as the bigger infant and junior school down the road, but make an effort to find out what it prides itself on and does best. In a smaller school, your visit may take the form of a meeting with the headteacher during the school day. Don't be intimidated by this. Remember that you are interviewing the headteacher – not the other way round! Prepare a few questions about what really interests you – whether this means swimming lessons or the school's policy on religion. This will make the

' Remember that you are interviewing the headteacher – not the other way round! '

point that you are a concerned and interested parent who wants to be involved in your child's education. As you go round the school, look at the way the teachers and children relate and try to get an impression of who is learning what in the classrooms that you visit.

One question you will have to answer for yourself is the best time to first visit the school. Do not be afraid to make an early visit. If you are sure that you will still be living in the area, going to see the headteacher when your child is three years old is a perfectly sensible thing to do. If you are unsure, ask the school secretary what most people do. It is often said that the secretary in a primary school knows more about what is going on than the headteacher and a helpful, cheerful and informative response is a good indicator of the state of the school as a whole.

Once you have made a decision, act quickly to secure the place. Don't just assume at the end of a visit that a place is arranged because you have put your name on a list. Write to the headteacher, confirming that you are delighted that your child is to attend the school from whatever date you have decided. If it is to be on a part-time basis, make that clear as well.

Finally, remember that writing this letter is the start of your family's involvement with the school. That involvement will give you rights as far as your child's education is concerned, but it also brings responsibilities. Once you have made this commitment, you should recognise the role of the school in your child's upbringing and you should appreciate how you can help to sustain the aims of the school through the home. Choosing a primary school should be seen as the start of a long and positive relationship that will be a major formative influence on your child.

Summing up

What you need to decide

- **Whether there is a genuine choice to be made**
- **What your priorities are**
- **What type of school would best suit your child**

What you need to do

- **Write to, or telephone, the school asking for a copy of the prospectus and the governing body's most recent report, and about visits and open days. Study the prospectus and report before you visit, so you are well prepared**
- **Look out for the evidence of a good school and don't be taken in by glossy prospectuses or stage-managed visits**
- **When you have chosen, act promptly, by writing to the school**

4 Starting school

Starting school can be a worrying time for both parents and children. It is important to talk about the school with your child from an early age and to make clear that it is something to be excited about. Many schools offer induction programmes, when children can go for part of a day to experience school life with parents at hand. If these are available, try to make use of them.

'The first days in a reception class are likely to be very exhausting'

However, the first days in a reception class are still likely to be, if nothing else, very exhausting for your child, and this can lead to emotional outbursts. Some children take to school immediately and never waver in their enthusiasm. Others start quietly, but then decide that organised education is not for them! Some cry from the start. Most have bad days as well as good. The important thing for parents to recognise is that there is no fail-safe way to introduce a child to school without tears and that whatever happens is commonplace as far as the reception class teacher is concerned.

On the first day, many schools will have special arrangements for the new intake. This normally means that parents deliver childen to the classroom rather than the gates. As a parent, it is useful if you know where you are going, as this will instil confidence in your child, so make sure you know what the arrangements are in advance. Most teachers will have a selection of entertaining activities on hand for the first few days of a new term. Reassuring as it is to stay and make sure that your child settles down with something, it may be better to disappear quite promptly and let the teacher take charge. A huge box of Lego and a play-house is often a better cure for nervous tears than a parent's – equally nervous – concern!

It is important to maintain interest in what your child is doing at school in the first few weeks. Teachers know this and will shower you with ragged paintings and monsters made of plastic cups. You should show great interest in these signs of independent activity and lavish praise on your child's efforts. If, after a few weeks, a child is still obviously unhappy about going to school it is worth having a chat with the reception class teacher. If you have both noticed the problem then you can work together to overcome it. Don't be surprised, however, if the teacher has seen no signs of unhappiness. A child can get into the habit of crying every morning but becomes a changed person once a parent has left him or her at the school gate!

Summing up

Before your child goes to school, it helps if he or she can:

- Dress and undress – including fastening shoes
- Go to the toilet unsupervised
- Wash and dry face and hands
- Eat tidily, using a knife and fork
- Tidy and clear away toys

- Use a handkerchief
- Mix with other children of the same age
- Respond to instructions given by adults
- Take an interest in picture books

5 The National Curriculum

HOW IT DEVELOPED

Today, it is difficult for anyone involved with schools to imagine working without the framework provided by the National Curriculum. Before 1988, what was taught in schools was up to the teachers who worked there. In practice, this meant that each school's curriculum was a mixture of tradition and habit. Then, and for the first time in our history, the 1988 Education Reform Act created a framework that stated legally what subjects should be taught in schools and to what standard.

Since then, that framework has developed into the National Curriculum we have today. Along the way there has been disagreement over exactly what should be taught and how it should be tested. But there should be no major changes to the existing system until at least the year 2000.

Although schools in the private sector do not have to follow the National Curriculum, many do so, at least as the minimum education for their pupils. For all other schools – LEA, voluntary aided, grant maintained and so forth – the National Curriculum forms the basis of pupils' education from ages 5-16.

HOW THE SCHOOL YEARS ARE ARRANGED

Under the National Curriculum, pupils' education is arranged in four phases, known as Key Stages. School year descriptions also have been standardised, with the first year of primary school now known as Year One. The table below shows you the relationship between Key Stages, school years and children's ages.

'Pupils' education is arranged in four phases, known as Key Stages'

Key stage	School year	Age
1	Y1	5-6
	Y2	6-7
2	Y3	7-8
	Y4	8-9
	Y5	9-10
	Y6	10-11
3	Y7	11-12
	Y8	12-13
	Y9	13-14
4	Y10	14-15
	Y11	15-16

The organisation of school year-groups under the National Curriculum

The National Curriculum for Key Stages 1 and 2 consists of ten subjects. Three of these – English, Mathematics and Science – are known as the **core subjects** because of their central importance. The other subjects are known as **foundation subjects** and include History, Geography, Design and Technology (including the old 'craft' subjects such as woodwork and needlework), Information Technology (the use of computers), Art, Music and Physical Education. Some primary schools may teach a modern foreign language (usually French) to older pupils, but studying a modern language is compulsory only from Key Stage 3. For pupils in Wales, the study of Welsh is also part of the National Curriculum.

THE TEACHING AND MONITORING OF SUBJECTS

All subjects are made up from **programmes of study**. These describe in detail what pupils should be taught for each Key Stage. The programmes of study set out the skills pupils should be developing and practising, the content they are expected to learn and the concepts they must understand. They do not, however, say *how* the subject should be taught. This is for teachers to decide. They will use the programmes of study to plan their own schemes of work.

To help monitor and judge pupils' progress, there are **attainment targets** for each subject. The titles of these reflect the titles of the programmes of study. Each attainment target is written as a series of **level descriptions**. These are used to judge a pupil's performance at the end of a Key Stage. They describe the types and range of performance which pupils working at a particular level should demonstrate. Teachers will use their knowledge of a pupil's work to judge which level description best fits his or her performance.

Across Key Stages 1-3 there are eight levels, plus a description of exceptional performance above Level 8. On average, a pupil is expected to advance one level for every two years at school. This is illustrated in the following chart.

Level	7 years of age (end of Key Stage 1)	11 years of age (end of Key Stage 2)	14 years of age (end of Key Stage 3)
Above Level 8			■ (exceptional)
Level 8			■ (exceeded)
Level 7			■ (exceeded)
Level 6		■ (achieved)	■ (achieved)
Level 5		■ (exceeded)	■ (achieved)
Level 4	■ (achieved)	■ (achieved)	
Level 3	■ (exceeded)		
Level 2	■ (achieved)		

■ = Achieved the target for the age group
■ = Exceeded the target for the age group
■ = Exceptional performance for the age group

Levels of achievement at the end of each Key Stage

All of this sounds complex but, once you understand the framework, it provides a way of talking about teaching and learning that is the same for all schools.

THE MAIN BENEFITS

' The level descriptions for each subject are linked '

Where this structure comes into its own is when a child moves from one school to another. An assessment for each subject using the nationally adopted level descriptions will give the new school some clear information about the standard that child has reached. Even when children only move from class to class within an infant and junior school, the new teacher can have, on a single sheet of paper, a detailed record of progress to date. Also, the level descriptions for each subject are linked so that, in broad terms, a Level 3 in English can be compared to a Level 3 in Science or Mathematics. This may help parents to identify where their children are under-achieving and guide them in giving help and support. At its simplest, finding out that your child has a higher level for writing than reading might suggest to you that you should encourage more reading at home.

These are the benefits of a common curriculum for all children but, as any parent knows, every child is different. So, while it is helpful to understand how the curriculum is structured, it is also important to remember that the compulsory curriculum can be delivered to pupils in a variety of ways and that children's learning often relies on their particular state of development and readiness.

Also, while subject levels can be helpful in indicating how groups of children are developing, they are only general indicators in assessment terms. It is vital that teachers and parents are positive about primary school achievements, and taking too much notice of levels is unlikely to help children do better. In fact, you are likely to find that most primary schools do not rely on levels but instead stress the positive aspects of their work through records of achievement that recognise, and reward, success.

Summing up

The structure of the National Curriculum

1 **Key Stages in primary schools**
   KS1 = Years One-Two = 5-7 year-olds
   KS2 = Years Three-Six = 7-11 year-olds
2 **National Curriculum subjects in primary schools**
   Core: English, Mathematics, Science
   Foundation: History, Geography,
   Design and Technology, Information Technology, Art, Music, Physical Education
3 **Average level of attainment expected at end of each Key Stage**
   KS1 = Level 2
   KS2 = Level 4

6 The primary school curriculum

When children first attend school, the teachers will have three main aims. The first is to develop the basic skills that allow children to learn other subjects. Developing these skills – reading, writing and number, sometimes called the 'three Rs' – is a major task for the primary school and, because of this, English and Mathematics are given extra teaching time in most primary schools.

Secondly, the teachers will also want to introduce the children to a range of interesting work in other subjects – providing a taster of the curriculum to come and arousing their interests. Finally, and very importantly, this is a time for children to develop positive attitudes to school and learning and the ability to work with others.

In some schools, **baseline assessments** are made at this time. In making a baseline assessment, the teacher checks how well children read and count and may give them simple aptitude tests. The results are used to help the school measure the subsequent progess made by a child – not as a check on the parents!

' Developing the 'three Rs' is a major task for the primary school '

Reading, writing and number work are expected to take up to 50% of the typical school week. The emphasis on number work comes by encouraging teachers to focus on the parts of the Mathematics curriculum concerned with number at the start of Key Stage 1. The pupil assessment at the end of Key Stage 1 focuses on these skills in particular. However, teachers are expected to cover all the other eight subjects as well. Typically, this might be for around 45 minutes a week per subject.

In Key Stage 2, the balance shifts slightly so that English and Mathematics take up around 40% of the curriculum time, leaving Science around two hours and the other subjects approximately one hour a week. By now, the English and Mathematics taught can go beyond the basic skills, but these should still be revised regularly. Within the typical primary school day, there are around four hours available for teaching after taking away registration, assemblies and breaks. If two hours is taken up with the basic skills, and plenty of time given to play, exercise and practical work, then it is clear that the other subjects will not be covered in great detail. However, the National Curriculum is only intended to take up 80% of the school week. That allows the school to use the remaining 20% as the headteacher and governors decide.

The policy of promoting the basic skills as a priority is an area where parents can support their children – perhaps by encouraging regular reading or making practical number work part of life at home. Twenty minutes a day 'working' with your child is almost the equivalent of another half a day at school a week.

In reading the subject details on the following pages, it is important to remember that teachers may sometimes have to decide what should be given most importance in their classrooms. Also, do not always expect to see evidence that everything in the curriculum has been covered. It would not be possible to cover every topic in History, for example, in great detail. The teacher may therefore decide to skate over some areas while providing extra depth in others.

ENGLISH

The programme of study and attainment targets in English cover three areas. These are: (1) **Speaking and Listening**, (2) **Reading** and (3) **Writing**. These skills are all equally important. Children who are not fluent speakers will always have difficulty in writing, while those children who enjoy reading are likely to become more sophisticated speakers. Teachers usually have a teaching scheme that includes these elements in linked ways. For example, it would be unusual to find a writing lesson going on that had not started with some talk or reading.

When children first start school, there is likely to be an immediate emphasis on reading. There is plenty of evidence to show that children learn to read at their own pace and in their own ways, so almost all schools have some kind of individualised reading programme. That makes the role of parents particularly important in supporting the reading work done in school. It is important to surround young children with books and to show that, as a parent, you both value and use books. As children go through primary school, the range of reading increases. The teacher will introduce the class to the media with time to discuss TV and magazines and there will be more opportunities to see how computers can help them with their work.

In Speaking and Listening, children are given opportunities to use talk in many different ways including telling stories, listening to poetry and reading aloud. They are given chances to talk about their experiences and to talk confidently to friends in the class, their teacher and other adults. They play word games and learn about the words associated with specific occasions, such as greetings or celebrations. They are taught to listen carefully. During the primary years, children are introduced to Standard English. This is the 'grammatically correct' English used in formal situations and, at this stage, teachers might, for example, discuss the difference between 'we was' and 'we were' or talk about how to greet a visitor to the school politely.

For Reading, the most important thing is that children read lots of stories and factual books. As their reading skills develop, older children are encouraged to use dictionaries, computer-based reference material and encyclopedias. The fiction they read can include poems and stories written by well-known children's authors and stories from a range of other countries and cultures. They should learn to read with fluency, accuracy and enjoyment. This includes learning the alphabet and using various approaches to reading including phonics – the sounds made by letters and by groups of letters. They will be encouraged to respond to their reading and to talk about characters, events and language in books, retell stories or say what might happen next.

In Writing, children are helped to understand the value of writing as a means of communicating and developing ideas and as a source of enjoyment. Even at Key Stage 1, children will be taught to write in different forms including stories and diaries. Children should learn to write with confidence, fluency and accuracy, with opportunities to plan and draft their writing. They will be given plenty of chances to work together, reading their work aloud and discussing it. They should be taught to use basic punctuation in their writing. In spelling, pupils should be taught to write each letter of the alphabet and to spell common words. In handwriting, pupils will learn the conventional ways of forming letters, 'joined-up' writing and how to hold a pencil comfortably. It is worth finding out when children are first taught to link handwriting so that you can encourage them to do the same at home.

MATHEMATICS

The programmes of study and attainment targets for Mathematics cover four areas. These are: (1) **Using and Applying Mathematics**, (2) **Number**, (3) **Shape, Space and Measures** and (4) **Handling Data**. Using and Applying Mathematics covers all of what might be called the practical side of Mathematics, from playing shops to talking about the relationships between shapes. Number includes what are called the four operations – addition, subtraction, multiplication and division. Shape, Space and Measures covers what used to be called geometry and more about areas and shapes. Handling Data covers tables, statistics and figures.

In the primary school, these should all be linked in the school's scheme of work with the main emphasis on number. In fact, at Key Stage 1, only Using and Applying Mathematics, Shape, Space and Measures and Number have to be taught. What this means in practice is that, while some of the words and methods have changed, the work your children do today is not that much different from what you encountered. Where it does differ is in its approach, so that there is much more problem-solving on the road to understanding and an emphasis on how Mathematics can be applied to everyday life. Many schools offer evenings where these changes are explained, so that parents can relate the Maths they did at school to that being done by their children.

In a typical classroom, Using and Applying Mathematics might involve learning mathematical terms and the idea that things are 'bigger' or 'smaller' than one another. Practical weighing or measuring exercises could follow. For Number, children have to be given opportunities to work with numbers, both orally and mentally. They may use calculators or computers to help them. They should be taught to count in different sequences, including odd and even numbers. They should learn their tables and practise addition, subtraction, multiplication and division. For Shape, Space and Measures, children could use programmable toys to measure turns and distance, or learn about circles, triangles and cubes.

As children go through primary school, they are encouraged to be more investigative in Mathematics. They will be asked to think about different mathematical approaches to tasks and taught to check their results. Decimals, fractions and percentages are taught in more detail. Graphs and co-ordinates are introduced and two-dimensional and three-dimensional shapes are investigated. Handling Data involves the design and interpretation of charts, tables, graphs and diagrams.

SCIENCE

The programmes of study and attainment targets for Science cover four areas. These are: (1) **Experimental and Investigative Science**, (2) **Life Processes and Living Things** (Biology), (3) **Materials and their Properties** (Chemistry) and (4) **Physical Processes** (Physics).

In the early years in primary school the main emphasis is on the three Rs, but pupils must do some science at a fairly simple level. The teacher will stress that science is about finding answers to questions about the world, like 'How?', 'Why?' and 'What will happen if...?' These questions are related to everyday life, personal health and living things. The teacher will also want to show the children how Science works by collecting observations and analysing evidence and, on the way, will be introducing scientific terms. One important aspect of Science in schools today is health and safety and the teacher will underline the possible hazards when working with some materials.

So, at Key Stage 1, pupils are expected to learn about the characteristics of living things and that animals, including humans, move, feed, grow, use their senses and reproduce. Along the way, they might think about how joints in the skeleton work, discuss the five senses and learn about the need for regular exercise. Alternatively, the teacher might set up a simple observation-based experiment. The pupils will be asked to think about what might happen and to turn their ideas into a form where they can be tested. They will then observe and make careful records before, finally, discussing or writing down their findings.

As children go through primary school, their work continues in a similar way, but with new materials and more complicated explanations. Simple scientific apparatus is likely to be introduced. The Science curriculum is so detailed that teachers will find it hard to complete everything and few pupils will master all of the information. It is more important that pupils start to understand the methods of Science and develop an enthusiasm for it. This is particularly so for girls, as there is clear evidence that many girls decide that Science is a boring, boys' subject long before they reach secondary school.

One point that all parents need to be aware of is that there is a major shortage of good Science teachers in primary schools and the National Curriculum for Science demands a lot from non-specialist teachers. While your children's school may be one of the lucky ones, there is a lot to be said for buying your children (especially girls) interesting books about Science from an early age and encouraging them to ask 'scientific' questions in the garden, kitchen and park.

DESIGN AND TECHNOLOGY

Design and Technology is a topic which combines all of the old practical subjects like cookery, woodwork and metalwork under a single umbrella. It has two simple attainment targets: (1) **Designing** and (2) **Making**. The basic idea behind this curriculum is the notion of using or combining materials to make something new. This definition could apply equally to an omelette, a small bookshelf or a radio. The emphasis is on investigating materials and their uses and looking at objects to see how they are made or how they work. Making drawings and models using different materials is a major part of this. It involves learning about ways to join materials, about wheels that make things mobile and joints that link components. It is also about how to make an object suit its purpose.

As children go through the school, the design process is emphasised. This may involve setting a problem and giving a group the chance to solve it. For example, building a raft that floats (from a limited choice of materials) involves finding out what materials are most buoyant and deciding how to link them with materials that do not dissolve in water. A teacher will encourage the class to think about designs, test them out and then decide how successful they were and what they might have done differently. Such an exercise involves drawing and planning as well as working with materials to shape them.

Design and Technology lessons should be popular with pupils. Research shows that one of the things children like best about primary school is making things as a team, so these lessons may also help to encourage the important skills of working together. In smaller schools, suitable areas for Design and Technology may be hard to find, but teachers should be willing to improvise; for example, it might be possible to do the major work in this area in the summer term, when the class could work outside. Parents should realise that it is unlikely that children will do work of this kind in every week of the school year.

INFORMATION TECHNOLOGY

Information Technology (IT) means the use of computers and related equipment. It is the only genuinely new subject in the National Curriculum. While computers might seem most appropriate to older children, teachers believe that if children start to use computer keyboards and programs at an early age they will be more at home with them in the technological age of the next century. The government has backed them with some cash so all primary schools should have at least one up-to-date computer for pupils to use. However, it is also true to say that few schools currently have enough of the most up-to-date equipment for all pupils to have the access to computing that their teachers would prefer.

The aim of the subject is not so much to create computer whizz-kids as to make pupils confident when they use new equipment and software and to give them an idea of the increasing importance of IT in the outside world.

Older children are taught to explore and solve the problems they encounter in other subjects and to use equipment and software to communicate ideas and information via text, graphs, pictures and sound. The emphasis is on making the best choice of software for a particular task and then using it appropriately. So, children may use word processors to help their writing or databases to record their findings in Science. For example, many primary schools now have computerised weather stations where observations (Science), measurement (Maths) and writing skills (English) all combine in its day-to-day operation.

HISTORY

History has only one attainment target – called History – but the subject has three main aims. These are: to give children an awareness of the past and how it was different from the present; to understand history as a sequence of events; and to explore some of the ways in which historians find out about the past.

Pupils should be taught about the everyday life of people in the past, about the lives of different kinds of famous men and women and about past events that are still remembered. As this takes place, they should also learn a sense of how changes take place over time and think about the reasons why people acted in certain ways. That should lead them on to consider different interpretations of history and to look at how to ask – and answer – questions about the past.

In Key Stage 2, pupils start a journey through history that takes them to the present day by the time they are 14 years old. This consists of study units, beginning with the Romans, Anglo-Saxons and Vikings in Britain. Later, five more study units are covered dealing with Life in Tudor Times, Life in Victorian Britain or in Britain since 1930, Ancient Greece, an aspect of local history, and a past non-European society. The curriculum gives a balance of British and world history and a mixture of political history (major events) and social history (how people lived).

The requirement to study an aspect of the local community is a new one. It could include something like the impact of the Norman Conquest, the local area during the Civil War or the impact of the First World War on a town. It gives the class a chance to 'do' History, perhaps by relating church records and graveyards with death rates among children in Victorian Britain as part of that study unit.

As with many other subjects, the amount of ground to be covered in History is enormous. Teachers have to skip over some areas if they are to find the time to devote to others in detail. You may find that your child's teacher will work on one project intensively for part of a term, rather than spread the teaching over a year.

GEOGRAPHY

Geography is split into three areas: (1) **Skills**, (2) **Places** and (3) **Themes**. Pupils are encouraged to investigate the main features of their surroundings and ask geographical questions such as 'Where is

it'? and 'How did it get like this'? Skills could be using the right words to describe features, following directions and making and using maps. A new skill is using what are known as secondary sources, such as pictures, aerial photographs, videos and CD-ROM encyclopedias, to find out information. In Places, the class is taught about the main features of an area and how its physical features and climate affect the lives of the people who live there. In Themes, the class explore how the environment is changing, or discuss issues like conservation.

Older pupils are encouraged to recognise patterns, such as variations in rainfall, and to make links between places through regional studies. They are expected to explore geographical questions by collecting and analysing evidence and to use instruments like rain gauges to make measurements. During Key Stage 2, three specific places have to be studied, including the locality of the school, one other area in the United Kingdom and another in a developing country elsewhere in the world. Like History, Geography only has limited curriculum time, so different teachers will spread the set work in different ways.

ART

Art and Music have always been popular subjects in the primary school. Art today means a lot more than painting and drawing and covers what might be termed art, craft and design. It has two attainment targets: (1) **Investigating and Making** and (2) **Knowledge and Understanding**. So teachers encourage activities that bring together three processes – investigating, making and knowledge. That can involve work on pattern and texture or on how colours are mixed, plus a chance to explore the work of artists and designers and to find out more about areas like photography, sculpture or architecture before the practical making exercise begins. In this sense, Art is a more structured lesson than it used to be: the teacher's scheme of work is organised to give a range of opportunities, possibly including the chance to visit art exhibitions.

MUSIC

The essential activities in Music are making music and appreciation. The subject has two attainment targets: (1) **Performing and Composing** and (2) **Listening and Appraising**. Children should be taught to sing songs from memory, play simple pieces and accompaniments, improvise and record their compositions. They are also expected to learn about the elements of music and about pitch and tempo. They should listen to music from different times and cultures and by well-known composers and performers.

For older children the opportunities are the same, but the level required is more advanced. Compositions should be more sophisticated and pupils should be able to identify the sounds made by instruments and discuss how sound can be used to communicate a mood or effect or how music reflects the time and place in which it was created. A wider range of listening should include music from different musical traditions and lead the pupils to develop their own ideas and opinions.

PHYSICAL EDUCATION

Physical Education is now a compulsory subject for all pupils and has three main aims. These are: to promote physical activity and healthy lifestyles; to develop positive attitudes; and to ensure the safety of those taking part. Children are taught to respond to instructions and to follow relevant rules and safety procedures. They learn about the safety risks of wearing inappropriate clothing and how to warm up for, and recover from, exercise.

The subject is divided into six areas of activity. For Key Stage 1, these are: Games, Gymnastic Activities and Dance. For Key Stage 2, Athletic Activities and Outdoor and Adventurous Activities are added. Teachers will probably spend most time on games, but dance – taught as movement – is compulsory for both boys and girls. Swimming, the sixth area of activity, can be taught at Key Stage 1 or Key Stage 2. The decision tends to depend on where the nearest facilities are situated. The requirements are quite specific and all pupils should be able to swim 25 metres by the end of their primary schooling.

FOREIGN LANGUAGES

The teaching of a modern foreign language is not required in UK primary schools, despite research from all over the world which shows that the earlier language learning begins, the more successful it is likely to be. However, some schools use the time allocated outside the National Curriculum to introduce a language – usually French – in the later years, to give pupils a useful grounding in the subject for secondary school. You should enquire about this when you visit the school.

RELIGIOUS EDUCATION

Although Religious Education (RE) is not a National Curriculum subject, it must be provided for all pupils. Parents have the right to withdraw their children from these lessons and teachers cannot be instructed to teach the subject. There should be around 40 hours of teaching per year in a typical primary school. There must also be a daily act of collective worship in the school which should be broadly Christian. A long debate over what should be taught in RE lessons ended with the publishing of what are known as 'model' syllabuses. To all intents and purposes, these are like National Curriculum subjects. They even have two attainment targets: (1) **Learning about Religion** and (2) **Learning from Religion**. However, they do not have to be followed exactly and can be modified. The result is that each school can have its own tailor-made version of Religious Education.

This is important in some multi-racial schools, where it is also possible to apply for permission to change the nature of the collective worship. However, in primary schools, it is quite unusual for children to be withdrawn from Religious Education as it is usually very general in nature and unlikely to offend.

SEX EDUCATION

Sex Education in schools has become a national issue since the 1993 decision that it should be a separate subject. This was done to allow parents the same right to withdraw their children from these lessons as from Religious Education. There is strong parental support for Sex Education in schools. In a recent survey, 94% of parents called for Sex Education lessons and 70% said they would not withdraw their children from them under any circumstances.

There is no set curriculum for Sex Education. Instead, every school must have a policy, approved by the governors, in line with 1994 national guidelines. In primary schools, the governors have the responsibility for deciding whether or not to include Sex Education in the curriculum. They are obliged to maintain a policy statement on the matter and this must be available to parents. All Sex Education must be provided within a spiritual and moral context. In practice, most primary schools do provide Sex Education classes, but not to all years. The lessons are focused on the physical and emotional changes involved in growing up. Parents are informed before they take place.

Summing up

Compulsory subjects in primary schools

SUBJECT	ATTAINMENT TARGETS	TIME PER WEEK AT KEY STAGE 1	TIME PER WEEK AT KEY STAGE 2
ENGLISH	3	5 hours	4 hours
MATHEMATICS	4	3 hours	3 hours
SCIENCE	4	90 minutes	2 hours
DESIGN AND TECHNOLOGY	2	45 minutes	1 hour
INFORMATION TECHNOLOGY	1	30 minutes	45 minutes
HISTORY	1	45 minutes	1 hour
GEOGRAPHY	1	45 minutes	1 hour
ART	2	45 minutes	1 hour
MUSIC	2	45 minutes	1 hour
PHYSICAL EDUCATION	Areas of activity	45 minutes	1 hour

Compulsory aspects of schooling, but not part of the National Curriculum

RELIGIOUS EDUCATION	2	45 minutes	1 hour
SEX EDUCATION	none	not specified	

7 Testing and assessment

THE PROCESS

Children are tested and assessed throughout their school careers. Teachers use tests to find out whether something that they have taught has been learned by their pupils. The results from these tests guide the teacher in making an assessment. Here all of a child's achievements, or achievements in a selected area, are looked at together.

CLASSROOM TESTS

' Tests can take place at any time '

Tests can take place at any time. Many people imagine that a test has to be written and carried out by an individual in silence but, in primary schools, tests are just as likely to be oral and carried out with the whole class. Tests are used for different purposes. Firstly, **regular classroom tests** can tell the teacher what he or she needs to repeat or practise with the class. They can diagnose the pupils' areas of weakness.

Sometimes a test, or tests, can sum up what has been learned over a period of time, ranging from a few lessons to the three or four years of a key stage. This kind of testing is called a **summative** assessment because it 'sums up' what the child has learned.

TEACHER ASSESSMENT

Teacher assessment is where the teacher uses his or her records and knowledge of a pupil to make an assessment. It is important to make the point that teacher assessments can say things about children that tests do not show. For example, a teacher assessment will note that a child who scores badly on an oral test may be shy and reserved, rather than ignorant of the right answer. Also, a child who works slowly or who panics in test situations is likely to be more accurately described by a teacher assessment.

Every child in a primary school is regularly assessed by his or her teachers. The teacher's record book contains informal assessments that the teacher has made as the child's activity is monitored as well as test results and marks or grades for particular pieces of work. These are the starting point for the teacher's regular reports to parents.

NATIONAL TESTING AND ASSESSMENT

From 1997, all children will be tested on entry to school; this is already done by some local authorities. The aim of this **baseline assessment** is to find out what each child can already do when he or she starts school in order to measure the subsequent success of the school and its teaching.

At the end of each Key Stage, a pupil's performance will be judged by a combination of national tests and formal teacher assessments. The national tests are held in May and are designed to provide a 'snapshot', objective judgement of a pupil's level of achievement. At the end of Key Stage 1, two subjects – English and Mathematics – are tested. At the end of Key Stage 2, Science is also tested.

Once the tests have been marked, the results are reported to parents. With the results of the tests, you will receive the results of the formal teacher assessments of work done in the classroom during the course of the year. You will also receive a summary of the results for all pupils in the school. This will help you to know how your child is doing compared with other children of the same age.

The current arrangements for testing at Key Stages 1 and 2 are described below, but the procedures are reviewed and revised each year. In the school year in which your child will be sitting the tests, your child's school will give you details of the arrangements in the autumn term. This means you will have plenty of time to help your child before May.

KEY STAGE ONE NATIONAL TESTS

At the end of Key Stage One, pupils will undergo a series of tasks and tests as part of the national testing. Tasks are classroom-based exercises; tests are written 'paper and pencil' exercises.

ENGLISH

In English, reading, writing and spelling are tested. There are classroom reading tasks for children at Levels 1-2 plus reading comprehension tests at Levels 2 and 3. For reading at Level 2, three sub-grades (A,B,C) give more definition. Then there is a writing task that covers Levels 1-3 and a spelling test for Levels 2-3.

MATHEMATICS

There is a Mathematics task covering Level 1 and a test with an emphasis on Number. The test covers Levels 2-3. At Level 2, three sub-grades (A,B,C) are used.

KEY STAGE TWO NATIONAL TESTS

At the end of Key Stage Two, pupils will take national tests in English, Mathematics and Science. Most pupils will take written test papers aimed at around Levels 3-6. Children with learning difficulties will do classrom-based tasks, aimed at Levels 1-2. Most pupils will do two test papers for each of Mathematics and Science, and three for English. All the test papers are marked outside the school by external examiners.

ENGLISH

Pupils are tested on four areas: Reading, Writing, Spelling and Handwriting. The levels achieved for each area are brought together to give an overall National Test level.

MATHEMATICS AND SCIENCE

In Mathematics, the following areas will be tested: Number, Algebra, Shape, Space and Measures, Handling Data. In 1997, a short mental arithmetic test will be piloted. If successful, it will be made compulsory in 1998. In Science, pupils will be tested on Life Processes and Living Things, Materials and their Properties and Physical Processes.

HELPING YOUR CHILD PREPARE FOR NATIONAL TESTS

Parents, particularly at Key Stage 2, often want to help their children prepare for tests and tasks. However, it is important to understand that the tests are not the same as an 'eleven-plus' and that children should not be made anxious about them.

Nevertheless, the results could have an influence on which teaching group a child is placed in at secondary school and might, in odd cases, support a parent's appeal over a secondary school place. Because of this, many parents encourage their children to practise for the tests using some of the published study guides and practice materials. If you do this, sit down and 'learn' with your child rather than expecting him or her to work through practice papers alone. Remember also that it is important for your child to get a good night's sleep beforehand and go to school with the proper equipment.

Summing up

Testing and assessment

- **Classroom tests help teachers to see where pupils still need help**
- **Teacher assessment is where the teacher uses his or her records and experience to say what a child has learned**

- **National tests compare children in different schools by setting the same tests for all of them**

8 Key issues for parents

BULLYING

There is some evidence, and enough hearsay and rumour, to make any parent feel concerned about the problem of bullying in primary schools and it would be foolish to pretend that it does not exist. What is important is that the school has a strategy for dealing with bullying which pupils and parents understand.

Bullying comes in a variety of forms. Children do form 'pecking orders' at various times: this can be a cruel process, but it may not amount to actual bullying. It is something that a teacher should keep a careful eye on, always offering individuals the chance to show in a positive way what they are best at. However, where bullying is systematic, involves groups 'ganging-up' on individuals, the extortion of sweets, equipment or money, or physical violence, the school should be told and should take action.

As a parent, you should not be prepared to tolerate bullying that is deliberate or continues over a few days. Watch out for the signs that a child is suddenly unhappy about going to school or starts pretending to be unwell. Many children will not admit to being bullied, so it is important to reassure them that this is a common problem that, once in the open, can be solved quite rapidly. The initial point of contact is the class teacher. He or she will probably have seen nothing of the incident, but you should expect the matter to be referred quickly to senior staff and dealt with openly.

Where the school has a policy on bullying, this should guide the action taken. If, as a parent, you are unhappy about what the school proposes to do, it is reasonable to ask for a copy of this policy document. In general, it is wise not to over-react and to play down a single incident but, if you feel that the school is not facing up to a wider problem, contact the chair of governors. In those circumstances, you will probably then find that other parents feel exactly as you do.

Very often the problems appear to be traceable to two or three individuals who are apparently 'out of control'. It is important to remember that the school is likely to be very well aware of such a situation and will be dealing with it through contact with parents or social workers. In such cases, the school may listen to you but will want – quite reasonably – to continue with a particular policy and give it a chance to succeed.

One situation that can emerge is the discovery that your child is the one doing the bullying! The main thing here is not to let your shock and embarrassment cause you to over-react. Being firm but calm is the best approach. You may want to discuss the situation with your child's class teacher or headteacher.

' It would be foolish to pretend that bullying does not exist '

27

CLASS SIZES

The fact that schools are under endless financial pressure, and that teachers' salaries are their major expenditure, means that large classes are likely to be a continuing problem. It is important to appreciate that large classes are not necessarily bad for the pupils in them. If the teacher recognises the problems and adjusts his or her teaching style to cope, then the number of pupils may not be relevant.

As a rule of thumb, primary schools usually have around 25 pupils to each teacher, but that ratio will include the headteacher and deputies. Teachers also need time for preparation, meetings and marking. A school will sometimes accept larger numbers in some years in order to ease the teaching burden in others.

In some schools, mixed-year classes are necessary. This may cause more anxieties for parents. Where they are introduced, it is important that the school explains the problem and its action and if this is not done, parents are entitled to ask why.

There is much that parents can do to support teachers facing large classes. Few teachers will reject the offer of some specific support, such as hearing pupils read or monitoring practical activities. As a parent, use your own expertise when you volunteer. If you like cooking, offer to cook; if you would rather be leading a painting group or organising some sport then volunteer to help in that way. Once you have volunteered, follow three simple rules: do not let the teacher down by not turning up; get on with your activity without bothering the teacher; and do not talk outside school about the pupils you encounter.

The other important thing to do is to support your child at home. Ask about what happened at school, suggest ideas for follow-up activities and monitor his or her schoolwork.

DISCIPLINE

Good discipline is essential if successful teaching and learning are to take place. However, be careful not to confuse discipline with matters like lining up in silence or filing out of the classroom. A disciplined class is one where the teaching and learning that is going on dictates how formal the class should be.

Nowadays, many schools have a policy on discipline that is agreed with parents. It is important that you can share the school's expectations of behaviour and promote them at home. Even where you may disagree with something the school does, it may be better not to say anything about it rather than encourage rebellion!

Recently, there has been controversy over the provision that schools have to make for children who are disruptive. If you have concerns about an individual who appears to be disrupting the work of your own child, you are quite entitled to raise this with the school.

SUPPORT FOR PUPILS WITH SPECIAL NEEDS

Around one-fifth of all school pupils are believed to have some kind of special educational need. This can range from having severe learning difficulties, a physical handicap or a minor difficulty with some aspect of learning like reading or number. The range of help available can vary from extra support in classrooms to the widening of doors for wheelchair access.

The principle behind this is that all pupils – whatever their disadvantages and disabilities – are entitled to go to the same schools and follow the same curriculum. This is a change in policy. Only a few years ago, these children were sent to special schools.

This has two consequences. The first is that your child may encounter other children with severe special needs and it is important to make sure that he or she is prepared for this. The second is that the way in which children are described as having special needs has changed. A child with a special need is now given what is called a 'statement' that says exactly what the special need is and what the school must do to help the child to cope with it. Different needs are given different levels of statement, but all are reviewed each year to see whether they still apply and whether the school has been successful in meeting the requirements of the statement.

It is most unlikely that a school would suggest statementing a child without the full co-operation of the parents at a much earlier stage. Sometimes, schools prefer not to statement pupils with minor needs and, instead, deal informally with overcoming the problem. It is important to stress that a statement is an entitlement for a pupil, not a way of labelling him or her as stupid or disabled. It is a document that makes sure the school does its legal duty on the child's behalf.

Summing up

How to raise a worry with the school:

- **For most matters, your first point of contact should be the class teacher. Talk to him or her first if you are worried about problems with friends or bullying, or if your child is having a problem in a particular area. Telephone the school and leave a message asking the class teacher to meet you at the end of the day or to call you back at a set time**

- **If the matter is sensitive in that it involves things you have been told in confidence that may or may not be true, such as an allegation against a teacher or criminal behaviour by someone, make an appointment with the school secretary to see the headteacher. If the matter is urgent, say so when you call**

9 How you can be involved

HOW TO GO ABOUT IT

All parents want to take part in their children's schooling, but are often unsure how to go about it. The starting point is that all parents come from different backgrounds. In a typical school community, there will be some people who know a lot about education, such as teachers who are having time out from their careers to bring up a family. There will be people who are involved in the community in other ways – perhaps as councillors or school governors. There will be people who work all day and only come to parents' evenings and there will also be people whose parents had no contact with their school and for whom schools are quite frightening places.

' There are many ways in which parents can be involved in their child's schooling '

The important thing about your involvement in the school is to decide how far you want to go. It is almost impossible nowadays to be uninvolved and few parents would want to miss the chance to talk to their child's teacher at a parents' meeting. This, and the individual's report, is still the main point of communication between teachers and parents, but it should not be the only one. Most primary school class teachers are approachable and, if you have something important to say or an anxiety you want to air, will always give you a few minutes at the end of the day. However, if you want to make a more formal point about something, you should make an appointment and expect to see the teacher with a senior member of staff.

There are many other ways in which parents have an opportunity to be involved with their child's schooling. First of all, it can simply be achieved by taking an interest in what your child has done each day and helping him or her to explore and carry forward what has been learned. Offering relevant trips to museums and places that have been mentioned in school shows that you value your child's education. Providing books and computers is a way of supporting the school at home and showing that yours is a family where learning is considered to be important. Finally, and perhaps most important of all, be on hand to give assistance with homework and projects.

However, there are four main ways in which you, as a parent, can actually take part in the life of the school:

THE GOVERNING BODY

Every school must have a governing body that includes between two and four parent governors. The actual number depends on the size of the school. Parent governors are elected by the parents for a four-year term and you will be notified when the election is due. There is a natural turnover of parent governors, because they must have children at the school when they are elected. So, it is quite reasonable to think about standing without suggesting that you are dissatisfied with the existing governors. To be elected, you will have to be nominated and then write a short note about why you think you are the best person to do the job. Experience of working with people, of handling money, or being typical of the school's locality in terms of where you live and work are more important than educational qualifications.

THE PARENT-TEACHER ASSOCIATION (PTA)

The PTA should be the school's best friend. It is a major source of funding for schools, and is often asked for advice by the governors. When your children are new to the school, the PTA may look very 'cliquey'. Go to meetings and become involved and you will find out that it is a place where people are all pulling together on behalf of the school. There may be a few people giving themselves airs and graces but if you spot this, you can be certain that others will too! PTAs sometimes have different names. You could find a 'Friends' association or a 'Home/School' organisation, but they all have a similar function.

CLASSROOM HELPING

Every school can use classroom helpers but remember the basic rules – never volunteer to do something you will not enjoy, never miss a week without telling the teacher in advance and do not talk about pupils outside the school. Remember that you are there to make space for the teacher, not to keep asking for equipment or support. If you are unsure about coping with children, you could offer to help in the school office.

CLASS TRIPS

The places that schools visit often have strict rules about the numbers of responsible adults that must accompany a primary school group. Offering to help can be a good way of getting to know your children's classmates, other parents and teachers without tying yourself down to a specific day each week.

Not everybody can find the time to be a governor, join the PTA, help in the classroom or go on trips. However, parents can still become involved with the school in other ways.

SCHOOL REPORTS AND PARENTS' MEETINGS

The annual school report is now a legal requirement. It must include comments on all National Curriculum subjects and details of national assessment results for children in Years Two and Six. There should be a note on overall progress and it should also invite parents to meet the teacher and follow up what is said. In fact, many primary schools report to parents on a termly or half-yearly basis.

THE SCHOOL PROSPECTUS

The school prospectus may have been a key factor in making your decision about which primary school to apply to. However, it is also an excellent way of keeping abreast of what is happening in the school. Among other information, it provides contact telephone numbers, advice on how the curriculum is taught, a summary of the sex education curriculum and information on national assessments. Parents should receive a copy each year.

SCHOOL INSPECTION

At present schools are inspected every four years. The process starts with a parents' evening where the school 'registered' inspector invites parents to complete a questionnaire and come to a meeting. The headteacher and staff are not allowed to attend that meeting and, if parents have worries, this is a chance to air them. It is a genuine opportunity – the school inspector is obliged by law to investigate the issues that parents raise and all parents have to be sent a summary of the inspector's report and are entitled to a free copy of the full report.

THE GOVERNORS' REPORT AND ANNUAL PARENTS' MEETING

Each year, the school governors have to publish an annual report for parents. Much of this is set down by law. It must contain details of all the governors, a financial statement, national assessment results and details of what the governors have attempted to achieve in the past year. It also includes an invitation to the annual parents' meeting.

This is one of the most important channels between parents and the governors. The meeting can pass resolutions that the governors must consider at their next meeting and can discuss anything that has involved the school in the previous year.

Summing up

So, with so many ways to be involved and the choice of being active or merely responding to school documents, there is a great opportunity for parents to have a clear idea of what is going on in their children's schools today. It is important to realise that being involved does not mean having to have specialised knowledge of the school or the educational system. What it does mean is that you have the will to help in the task of making your children's school a better – and happier – learning environment